Easy Canadian Cookbook

Authentic Canadian Cooking

By
Chef Maggie Chow
Copyright © by Saxonberg Associates
All rights reserved

Published by
BookSumo, a division of Saxonberg Associates
http://www.booksumo.com/

INTRODUCTION

Welcome to *The Effortless Chef Series*! Thank you for taking the time to download the *Easy Canadian Cookbook*. Come take a journey with me into the delights of easy cooking. The point of this cookbook and all my cookbooks is to exemplify the effortless nature of cooking simply.

In this book we focus on Canadian meals. You will find that even though the recipes are simple, the taste of the dishes is quite amazing.

So will you join me in an adventure of simple cooking? If the answer is yes (and I hope it is) please consult the table of contents to find the dishes you are most interested in. Once you are ready jump right in and start cooking.

— Chef Maggie Chow

Table of Contents

Introduction 2
Table of Contents 3
Any Issues? Contact Me 8
Legal Notes 9
Common Abbreviations 10
Chapter 1: Easy Canadian Recipes 11
   Raisin Tarts 11
   Buttered Roasted Turkey 13
   Fried Spicy Chicken 15
   Prosciutto Wrapped Pesto Chicken 18
   Stuffed Mushroom Caps 20
   Spicy Buttered Trout 22
   Herbed Meat Pie 24
   Maple Leaf Ham 27

- Cream Cheese Stuffed Mushrooms ... 29
- Avocado & Tomato Dip ... 31
- Hot Cheesy Chicken Dip ... 33
- Sweet Bacon Canadian Snacks ... 35
- Spicy Pulled Pork ... 37
- Canadian Asian Rice and Beef ... 39
- Baked Blueberry & Coconut Oatmeal ... 42
- Buttered Garlicky Potatoes ... 45
- Cheesy Spaghetti in Rosemary Sauce ... 47
- Grilled Herbed Veggies ... 49
- Brown Butter Spiced Banana Bread ... 51
- Chilled Creamy Broccoli Salad ... 53
- Pesto Spinach and Tomatoes ... 55
- Roasted Cauliflower, Garlic, and Leek Soup ... 57
- Chicken & Mushroom Kabobs with Rice ... 60
- Shawarma ... 63
- Buttered Apple Scones ... 66

Moist Egg Pancakes 69

Tangy Swordfish 71

Herbed Cheesy Sandwich 73

Sweet & Sour Pork with Bell Peppers 75

Bacon Wrapped Partridge Breasts 78

Potato Fries with Gravy 81

Cabbage Rolls in Tomato Gravy 83

Coconut & Raisin Tart 86

Nova Scotia Quiche 89

Moist Corn Fritters 92

Garlicky & Lemony Mayo 94

Beer & Spices Braised Shrimp 96

Tangy Prawns 98

Canadian BBQ Sauce 100

Baked Pollock with Veggies 102

Chicken & Sliders in Broth Gravy 104

Raisin Pudding 107

Mushroom Pastries	109
Crispy Smelts	111
Simple Shepherd's Pie	113
Cheesy Smoked Meat Tortilla	116
Creamy Lobster Sandwich	118
Spiced Meatballs Stew	120
Cheesy Spaghetti	123
Cheesy Lobster in Creamy Sauce	126
Delicious Apple Crisp	129
Meat Pie in Quebec Style	131
Quebec Cheesy French Fries	134
British Columbian Dessert	136
Classic Canadian Fried Pastries	139
Summertime Beet Soup	142
Old-Fashioned Dumplings	144
Wonderful Cabbage Casserole	147
Quintessential Canadian Tarts	149

Authentic Salmon Jerky 152

Springtime Lemony Fiddleheads 154

Traditional Newfoundland Meal 156

Family Feast Apple Crisp 158

THANKS FOR READING! NOW LET'S TRY SOME **SUSHI** AND **DUMP DINNERS**.... 160

Come On... 162

Let's Be Friends :) 162

Can I Ask A Favour? 163

Interested in Other Easy Cookbooks? 164

Any Issues? Contact Me

If you find that something important to you is missing from this book please contact me at maggie@booksumo.com.

I will try my best to re-publish a revised copy taking your feedback into consideration and let you know when the book has been revised with you in mind.

:)

— Chef Maggie Chow

LEGAL NOTES

ALL RIGHTS RESERVED. NO PART OF THIS BOOK MAY BE REPRODUCED OR TRANSMITTED IN ANY FORM OR BY ANY MEANS. PHOTOCOPYING, POSTING ONLINE, AND / OR DIGITAL COPYING IS STRICTLY PROHIBITED UNLESS WRITTEN PERMISSION IS GRANTED BY THE BOOK'S PUBLISHING COMPANY. LIMITED USE OF THE BOOK'S TEXT IS PERMITTED FOR USE IN REVIEWS WRITTEN FOR THE PUBLIC AND/OR PUBLIC DOMAIN.

COMMON ABBREVIATIONS

C.(s)	C.
tbsp	tbsp
tsp	tsp
oz.	oz.
lb	lb

*All units used are standard American measurements

Chapter 1: Easy Canadian Recipes

Raisin Tarts

Ingredients

- 16 (3 inch) unbaked tart shells
- 1 C. raisins
- 3/4 C. brown sugar
- 1/4 C. butter, softened
- 2 eggs
- 1/2 C. maple syrup
- 1 tbsp all-purpose flour
- 1 tbsp vanilla extract
- pinch of salt

Directions

- Set your oven to 350 degrees F before doing anything else.
- Place the raisins in the bottom of the tart shells evenly and arrange the shells onto a large baking sheet.
- In a bowl, add the butter and sugar and beat till smooth.
- Add the remaining ingredients and beat till well combined and transfer the mixture into the tart shells so they are about 3/4 full.
- Cook everything in the oven for about 16 minutes, turning the baking sheet once half way.

Amount per serving (16 total)

Timing Information:

Preparation	15 m
Cooking	20 m
Total Time	35 m

Nutritional Information:

Calories	258 kcal
Fat	10 g
Carbohydrates	40.7g
Protein	2.6 g
Cholesterol	31 mg
Sodium	133 mg

* Percent Daily Values are based on a 2,000 calorie diet.

BUTTERED ROASTED TURKEY

Ingredients

- 1 (18 lb) whole turkey
- 1/2 C. unsalted butter, softened
- salt and freshly ground black pepper to taste
- 1 1/2 quarts turkey stock
- 8 C. prepared stuffing

Directions

- Set your oven to 325 degrees F before doing anything else and arrange the rack in the lowest position of the oven. Now arrange a rack into a large roasting pan. Remove the neck and giblets from the turkey and then rinse and pat dry the turkey completely.
- Arrange the turkey, breast side up over the rack in the roasting pan and stuff the body cavity with stuffing loosely.
- Coat the skin of the turkey with the butter evenly and sprinkle with the salt and black pepper.
- Cover the turkey with foil and place 2 C. of the broth in the roasting pan.
- Roast for about 2 1/2 hours, basting and adding 1-2 C. of the broth after every 30 minutes.
- Remove the foil paper and cook for 1 1/2 hours more.
- Place the turkey onto a large cutting board for about 20-30 minutes before slicing.

Amount per serving (24 total)

Timing Information:

Preparation	30 m
Cooking	4 h
Total Time	4 h 30 m

Nutritional Information:

Calories	663 kcal
Fat	33.8 g
Carbohydrates	13.7g
Protein	72.2 g
Cholesterol	1211 mg
Sodium	710 mg

* Percent Daily Values are based on a 2,000 calorie diet.

Fried Spicy Chicken

Ingredients

- oil for deep frying
- 1 C. unbleached all-purpose flour
- 2 tsps salt
- 1/2 tsp ground black pepper
- 1/2 tsp cayenne pepper
- 1/4 tsp garlic powder
- 1/2 tsp paprika
- 1 egg
- 1 C. milk
- 3 skinless, boneless chicken breasts, cut into 1/2-inch strips
- 1/4 C. hot pepper sauce
- 1 tbsp butter

Directions

- In a shallow dish, add the milk and egg and beat till well combined.
- In another shallow dish, mix together the flour, garlic powder, paprika, cayenne pepper, salt and black pepper.
- Dip the chicken strips in the milk mixture and then coat them with the flour mixture evenly.
- Repeat this process for a double coating and refrigerate the strips for about 20 minutes.
- Meanwhile in a large pan or deep fryer, heat the oil to 375 degrees F.
- Carefully add the chicken strips into the hot oil and fry for about 5-6 minutes or till browned nicely.

- In a microwave safe bowl, mix together the butter and hot pepper sauce and microwave on high for about 20-30 seconds or till melted.
- Add the chicken strips and sauce into a bowl and stir to combine before serving.

Amount per serving (3 total)

Timing Information:

Preparation	10 m
Cooking	20 m
Total Time	50 m

Nutritional Information:

Calories	710 kcal
Fat	46.9 g
Carbohydrates	43.7g
Protein	28 g
Cholesterol	136 mg
Sodium	2334 mg

* Percent Daily Values are based on a 2,000 calorie diet.

Prosciutto Wrapped Pesto Chicken

Ingredients

- 4 skinless, boneless chicken breast halves
- 1/2 C. prepared basil pesto, divided
- 4 thin slices prosciutto, or more if needed

Directions

- Set your oven to 400 degrees F before doing anything else and grease a baking dish.
- Spread the pesto over the chicken breasts evenly and then with a piece of prosciutto wrap each breast.
- Arrange the breasts into the prepared baking dish in a single layer.
- Cook everything in the oven for about 25 minutes or till the desired doneness.

Amount per serving (4 total)

Timing Information:

Preparation	10 m
Cooking	25 m
Total Time	35 m

Nutritional Information:

Calories	312 kcal
Fat	19.3 g
Carbohydrates	2g
Protein	31.5 g
Cholesterol	83 mg
Sodium	434 mg

* Percent Daily Values are based on a 2,000 calorie diet.

Stuffed Mushroom Caps

Ingredients

- 1/4 C. butter
- 2 cloves garlic, minced
- 6 peeled and deveined large shrimp
- 6 mushrooms, stems removed
- 2 tbsps shredded mozzarella cheese

Directions

- Set your oven to 325 degrees F before doing anything else and lightly grease a 9x5-inch baking dish.
- In a skillet, melt the butter with garlic on medium heat and cook the shrimp for about 3 minutes.
- In each mushroom cap, place 1 shrimp and arrange into the prepared baking dish.
- Place the garlic butter from the skillet over the mushroom cap and top with cheese evenly.
- Cook everything in the oven for about 10-15 minutes or till the top becomes golden brown and bubbly.

Amount per serving (3 total)

Timing Information:

Preparation	15 m
Cooking	15 m
Total Time	30 m

Nutritional Information:

Calories	123 kcal
Fat	11 g
Carbohydrates	1.5g
Protein	5.1 g
Cholesterol	33 mg
Sodium	241 mg

* Percent Daily Values are based on a 2,000 calorie diet.

Spicy Buttered Trout

Ingredients

- 1 tbsp paprika
- 2 tsps dry mustard
- 1 tsp cayenne pepper
- 1 tsp ground cumin
- 1 tsp black pepper
- 1 tsp white pepper
- 1 tsp dried thyme
- 1 tsp salt
- 3/4 C. unsalted butter, melted
- 6 (4 oz.) fillets trout
- 1/4 C. unsalted butter, melted

Directions

- In a bowl, mix together the mustard, spices, thyme and salt.
- Heat a heavy cast iron skillet on high heat for about 10 minutes.
- In a shallow dish, place the melted butter.
- Coat each trout fillet with the butter and sprinkle with the spice mixture evenly.
- Add the trout fillets into the hot skillet in batches.
- Pour 1 tsp of melted butter on each fillet and cook for about 2 minutes.
- Flip and pour 1 tsp over each fillet and cook till desired doneness.
- Repeat with the remaining fillets.

Amount per serving (6 total)

Timing Information:

Preparation	20 m
Cooking	10 m
Total Time	30 m

Nutritional Information:

Calories	420 kcal
Fat	35.3 g
Carbohydrates	1.8g
Protein	24.3 g
Cholesterol	148 mg
Sodium	428 mg

* Percent Daily Values are based on a 2,000 calorie diet.

Herbed Meat Pie

Ingredients

- 1 lb lean ground pork
- 1/2 lb lean ground beef
- 1 onion, diced
- 1 clove garlic, minced
- 1/2 C. water
- 1 1/2 tsps salt
- 1/2 tsp dried thyme, crushed
- 1/4 tsp ground sage
- 1/4 tsp ground black pepper
- 1/8 tsp ground cloves
- 1 recipe pastry for a 9 inch double crust pie

Directions

- Set your oven to 425 degrees F before doing anything else.
- In a pan, mix together the beef, pork, onion, garlic, sage, thyme, cloves, salt, black pepper and water on medium heat and bring to a boil.
- Cook, stirring occasionally till the mixture starts to boil and then reduce the heat to low.
- Simmer for about 5 minutes and remove everything from the heat and let it cool.
- Now, transfer the meat mixture into the pie crust evenly and cover with the top crust.
- Seal the pie by pinching the edges and make slits in the top crust so steam can escape.

- With the strips of foil, cover the edges of the pie and cook everything in the oven for about 15-20 minutes or till the top becomes golden brown.
- Remove everything from the oven and keep it aside for about 10 minutes before slicing.

Amount per serving (8 total)

Timing Information:

Preparation	40 m
Cooking	40 m
Total Time	2 h

Nutritional Information:

Calories	405 kcal
Fat	26.6 g
Carbohydrates	22.1g
Protein	18.4 g
Cholesterol	55 mg
Sodium	749 mg

* Percent Daily Values are based on a 2,000 calorie diet.

Maple Leaf Ham

Ingredients

- 1 (5 lb) fully-cooked, bone-in ham
- 1/4 C. maple syrup
- 1 tbsp red wine vinegar
- 2 tbsps Dijon mustard
- 1 tbsp dry mustard

Directions

- Set your oven to 325 degrees F before doing anything else.
- With a sharp knife, trim off the excess fat from the ham and then make shallow cuts about 1-inch apart to score in a diamond pattern.
- Arrange the ham in a roasting pan and cook everything in the oven for about 30 minutes.
- Meanwhile in a bowl, mix together the remaining ingredients.
- Coat the ham with the glaze and continue cooking it for about 20 minutes, coating with the glaze twice.
- Remove everything from the oven and keep it aside for about 10-15 minutes before slicing.

Amount per serving (8 total)

Timing Information:

Preparation	15 m
Cooking	1 h 30 m
Total Time	1 h 45 m

Nutritional Information:

Calories	581 kcal
Fat	38.1 g
Carbohydrates	7.8g
Protein	48.7 g
Cholesterol	139 mg
Sodium	2758 mg

* Percent Daily Values are based on a 2,000 calorie diet.

Cream Cheese Stuffed Mushrooms

Ingredients

- 1/2 C. chopped green onions
- 2 (8 oz.) packages cream cheese, softened
- 20 fresh mushrooms, stems removed
- 1 lb sliced bacon, cut in half

Directions

- Set your oven to 350 degrees F before doing anything else.
- In a bowl, add the cream cheese and green onion and mix till well combined.
- Stuff the each mushroom cap with the cream cheese mixture evenly.
- With a piece of the bacon slice, wrap the each mushroom cap and secure with toothpicks.
- Arrange the mushroom caps into a baking sheet in a single layer and Cook everything in the oven for about 20 minutes.

Amount per serving (20 total)

Timing Information:

Preparation	10 m
Cooking	20 m
Total Time	30 m

Nutritional Information:

Calories	123 kcal
Fat	11 g
Carbohydrates	1.5g
Protein	5.1 g
Cholesterol	33 mg
Sodium	241 mg

* Percent Daily Values are based on a 2,000 calorie diet.

Avocado & Tomato Dip

Ingredients

- 3 avocados, peeled, pitted, and mashed
- 1 lime, juiced
- 1 tsp salt
- 1/2 C. diced onion
- 3 tbsps chopped fresh cilantro
- 2 roma tomatoes, diced
- 1 tsp minced garlic
- 1 pinch ground cayenne pepper

Directions

- In a large bowl, mix together all the ingredients.
- Serve immediately or you can refrigerate, covered for at least 1 hour for better flavor.

Amount per serving (4 total)

Timing Information:

Preparation	10 m
Cooking	10 m
Total Time	10 m

Nutritional Information:

Calories	262 kcal
Fat	22.2 g
Carbohydrates	18g
Protein	3.7 g
Cholesterol	0 mg
Sodium	596 mg

* Percent Daily Values are based on a 2,000 calorie diet.

Hot Cheesy Chicken Dip

Ingredients

- 2 (10 oz.) cans chunk chicken, drained
- 2 (8 oz.) packages cream cheese, softened
- 1 C. Ranch dressing
- 3/4 C. pepper sauce
- 1 1/2 C. shredded Cheddar cheese
- 1 bunch celery, cleaned and cut into 4 inch pieces
- 1 (8 oz.) box chicken-flavored crackers

Directions

- In a skillet, add the chicken and hot sauce on medium heat and cook till heated completely.
- Stir in the ranch dressing and cream cheese and cook stirring continuously till warmed and stir in half of the cheddar cheese.
- Immediately, transfer the mixture into a slow cooker and top with the remaining cheese.
- Set the slow cooker on Low and cook, covered for about 40 minutes or till bubbly.
- Serve hot with the crackers and celery sticks.

Amount per serving (20 total)

Timing Information:

Preparation	5 m
Cooking	40 m
Total Time	45 m

Nutritional Information:

Calories	284 kcal
Fat	22.6 g
Carbohydrates	8.6g
Protein	11.1 g
Cholesterol	54 mg
Sodium	552 mg

* Percent Daily Values are based on a 2,000 calorie diet.

Sweet Bacon Canadian Snacks

Ingredients

- 1 lb bacon
- 1 (16 oz.) package little smokie sausages
- 1 C. brown sugar, or to taste

Directions

- Set your oven to 350 degrees F before doing anything else.
- Cut the bacon slices into three pieces.
- Wrap each sausage with a piece of the bacon and thread onto pre-soaked wooden skewers.
- On a baking sheet, place the skewers in a single layer and sprinkle with brown sugar generously.
- Cook everything in the oven till the brown sugar is melted and the bacon becomes crisp.

Amount per serving (12 total)

Timing Information:

Preparation	10 m
Cooking	20 m
Total Time	30 m

Nutritional Information:

Calories	356 kcal
Fat	27.2 g
Carbohydrates	18.9g
Protein	9 g
Cholesterol	49 mg
Sodium	696 mg

* Percent Daily Values are based on a 2,000 calorie diet.

Spicy Pulled Pork

Ingredients

- 1 tsp salt
- 1 tsp garlic powder
- 1 tsp ground cumin
- 1/2 tsp crumbled dried oregano
- 1/2 tsp ground coriander
- 1/4 tsp ground cinnamon
- 1 (4 lb) boneless pork shoulder roast
- 2 bay leaves
- 2 C. chicken broth

Directions

- In a large bowl, mix together the salt, oregano and the spices and rub the pork with the spice mixture generously.
- In the bottom of a slow cooker, place the bay leaves topped by the pork.
- Carefully, add the broth around the pork.
- Set the slow cooker on Low and cook, covered for about 10 hours or till fork tender, flipping the pork once half way.
- Transfer the pork into a large bowl and with 2 forks, and shred it.
- You can use cooking liquid to moisten the pork meat.

Amount per serving (10 total)

Timing Information:

Preparation	10 m
Cooking	10 h
Total Time	10 h 10 m

Nutritional Information:

Calories	223 kcal
Fat	13.8 g
Carbohydrates	0.7g
Protein	22.2 g
Cholesterol	73 mg
Sodium	474 mg

* Percent Daily Values are based on a 2,000 calorie diet.

Canadian Asian Rice and Beef

Ingredients

- 1 1/2 lbs beef top sirloin, thinly sliced
- 1/3 C. white sugar
- 1/3 C. rice wine vinegar
- 2 tbsps frozen orange juice concentrate
- 1 tsp salt
- 1 tbsp soy sauce
- 1 C. long grain rice
- 2 C. water
- 1/4 C. cornstarch
- 2 tsps orange zest
- 3 tbsps grated fresh ginger
- 1 1/2 tbsps minced garlic
- 8 broccoli florets, lightly steamed
- 2 C. oil for frying

Directions

- Line a large baking sheet with paper towels.
- Arrange the beef strips onto the prepared baking sheet in a single layer and refrigerate for about 30 minutes.
- In a small bowl, mix together sugar, orange juice concentrate, vinegar, soy sauce and salt and keep aside.
- In a pan, mix together water and rice and bring to a boil.
- Reduce the heat to medium-low and simmer for about 20 minutes or till tender.
- In a skillet, heat oil on medium-high heat.

- Coat the beef with the cornstarch evenly and cook the beef in the skillet till golden brown and crispy and transfer onto a plate.
- Discard the fat from the skillet, leaving 1 tbsp.
- Add the garlic, ginger and orange zest and cook till fragrant.
- Stir in the vinegar mixture and bring to a simmer and cook for about 5 minutes or till the sauce become thick.
- Stir in the beef and cook till heated completely.
- Place the rice onto serving plates and top it with the beef mixture.
- Serve with a garnishing of broccoli.

Amount per serving (6 total)

Timing Information:

Preparation	20 m
Cooking	15 m
Total Time	1 h 5 m

Nutritional Information:

Calories	507 kcal
Fat	18.7 g
Carbohydrates	59.2g
Protein	27.4 g
Cholesterol	61 mg
Sodium	649 mg

* Percent Daily Values are based on a 2,000 calorie diet.

BAKED BLUEBERRY & COCONUT OATMEAL

Ingredients

- 2 C. rolled oats
- 1 C. unsweetened flaked coconut
- 1/4 C. light brown sugar
- 1 tsp baking powder
- 1 tsp ground cinnamon
- 1/2 tsp salt
- 2 C. skim milk
- 1 large egg, beaten
- 3 tbsps coconut oil, softened
- 1 tsp vanilla extract
- 1 1/2 C. blueberries

Directions

- Set your oven to 350 degrees F before doing anything else and grease an 8-inch baking dish.
- In a large bowl, mix together coconut, oats, baking powder, brown sugar, cinnamon and salt.
- In another bowl, add the remaining ingredients except blueberries and beat till well combined.

- In the bottom of the prepared baking dish, place about 2/3 of the blueberries evenly.
- Place the oat mixture over the blueberries evenly followed by the egg mixture.
- Top everything with the remaining blueberries evenly and cook it all in the oven for about 40 minutes.
- Remove everything from the oven and let it cool for about 5 minutes before serving.

Amount per serving (5 total)

Timing Information:

Preparation	10 m
Cooking	40 m
Total Time	55 m

Nutritional Information:

Calories	422 kcal
Fat	23.7 g
Carbohydrates	45.4g
Protein	10.5 g
Cholesterol	39 mg
Sodium	397 mg

* Percent Daily Values are based on a 2,000 calorie diet.

BUTTERED GARLICKY POTATOES

Ingredients

- 8 medium red potatoes, cubed
- 3 tbsps butter, melted
- 1 tbsp chopped fresh dill
- 2 tsps minced garlic
- 1/4 tsp salt

Directions

- Arrange a steamer basket over a pan of boiling water.
- Place the potatoes in the steamer basket and cook, covered for about 10 minutes or till the potatoes are just tender.
- Drain the potatoes well and transfer into a bowl.
- In a 2nd bowl, mix together remaining ingredients and transfer into the 1st bowl with the potatoes and mix well.

Amount per serving (5 total)

Timing Information:

Preparation	10 m
Cooking	10 m
Total Time	20 m

Nutritional Information:

Calories	330 kcal
Fat	7.2 g
Carbohydrates	62.1g
Protein	5.9 g
Cholesterol	18 mg
Sodium	178 mg

* Percent Daily Values are based on a 2,000 calorie diet.

Cheesy Spaghetti in Rosemary Sauce

Ingredients

- 6 tbsps unsalted butter, divided
- 1/2 C. finely chopped onion
- 6 cloves garlic, coarsely chopped
- 1 C. chicken broth
- 2 tbsps chopped fresh rosemary
- 1 (16 oz.) package spaghetti
- 1/4 C. grated Parmesan cheese
- kosher salt and cracked black pepper to taste

Directions

- In a large skillet, melt 1/4 C. of the butter on low heat and sauté the onion for about 10 minutes.
- Add garlic and sauté for about 2 minutes and stir in rosemary and chicken broth.
- Increase the heat to medium-high and cook for about 8 minutes or till the mixture reduces by 1/3.
- Meanwhile in a large pan of lightly salted boiling water, cook the spaghetti for about 8 minutes.
- Drain the spaghetti completely and add into the skillet and gently, stir to combine.
- Stir in the Parmesan, remaining butter, salt and black pepper and remove from heat.
- Serve hot with a garnishing of rosemary and extra parmesan.

Amount per serving (8 total)

Timing Information:

Preparation	10 m
Cooking	20 m
Total Time	30 m

Nutritional Information:

Calories	305 kcal
Fat	10.3 g
Carbohydrates	43.9g
Protein	8.8 g
Cholesterol	26 mg
Sodium	214 mg

* Percent Daily Values are based on a 2,000 calorie diet.

Grilled Herbed Veggies

Ingredients

- 2 tbsps olive oil
- 2 tbsps chopped fresh parsley
- 2 tbsps chopped fresh oregano
- 2 tbsps chopped fresh basil
- 1 tbsp balsamic vinegar
- 1 tsp kosher salt
- 1/2 tsp black pepper
- 6 cloves garlic, minced
- 1 red onion, cut into wedges
- 18 spears fresh asparagus, trimmed
- 12 crimini mushrooms, stems removed
- 1 (1 lb) eggplant, sliced into 1/4 inch rounds
- 1 red bell pepper, cut into wedges
- 1 yellow bell pepper, cut into wedges

Directions

- In a large resealable bag, add oil, vinegar, fresh herbs, garlic, salt and pepper and shake to mix.
- Add the vegetables and tightly, seal the bag and refrigerate to marinate for about 2 hours, flipping occasionally.
- Set your grill to high heat and grease the grill grate.
- Cook the vegetables on the grill for about 12 minutes, flipping once half way.

Amount per serving (6 total)

Timing Information:

Preparation	15 m
Cooking	12 m
Total Time	2 h 30 m

Nutritional Information:

Calories	107 kcal
Fat	4.9 g
Carbohydrates	13.3g
Protein	4.3 g
Cholesterol	0 mg
Sodium	340 mg

* Percent Daily Values are based on a 2,000 calorie diet.

Brown Butter Spiced Banana Bread

Ingredients

- 1/2 C. butter
- 3 very ripe bananas
- 1/4 C. brown sugar
- 1/4 C. white sugar
- 1 egg
- 1 tbsp vanilla extract
- 1 1/2 C. all-purpose flour
- 1 1/2 tsps baking soda
- 1 tsp ground cinnamon
- 1/2 tsp ground nutmeg

Directions

- In a small pan, melt butter on medium heat and cook, stirring continuously for about 5-10 minutes or till browned. Remove from heat and keep aside to cool for about 15 minutes. After cooling, transfer about 1/3 C. of the butter in a bowl for use. Meanwhile, set your oven to 350 degrees F before doing anything else and grease a loaf pan.
- In a large bowl, add the bananas and mash them completely.
- In the bowl of bananas, add 1/3 C. of brown butter, egg, both sugars and vanilla extract and mix till well combined.
- In another bowl, mix together flour, baking soda and spices.
- Add the flour mixture into the banana mixture and mix till well combined.
- Transfer the mixture onto the prepared loaf pan evenly and Cook everything in the oven for about 45 minutes or till a toothpick inserted in the center comes out clean.

Amount per serving (6 total)

Timing Information:

Preparation	15 m
Cooking	50 m
Total Time	1 h 20 m

Nutritional Information:

Calories	389 kcal
Fat	16.8 g
Carbohydrates	55.4g
Protein	5.1 g
Cholesterol	72 mg
Sodium	439 mg

* Percent Daily Values are based on a 2,000 calorie diet.

Chilled Creamy Broccoli Salad

Ingredients

- 3 C. broccoli florets
- 1/2 C. chopped red onion
- 1/4 C. sunflower seeds
- 1/2 C. chopped raisins
- 1/2 C. crumbled feta cheese
- 1/2 C. plain low-fat yogurt
- 1/4 C. light mayonnaise
- 2 tbsps white sugar
- 1 tbsp lemon juice
- salt and pepper to taste

Directions

- In a large bowl, mix together broccoli, onion, raisins, sunflower seeds and feta cheese.
- In another bowl, add the remaining ingredients and beat till well combined.
- Add the yogurt mixture into a salad bowl and toss to coat well.
- Refrigerate, covered for at least 2 hours.

Amount per serving (6 total)

Timing Information:

Preparation	25 m
Cooking	2 h 25 m
Total Time	25 m

Nutritional Information:

Calories	119 kcal
Fat	3.2 g
Carbohydrates	20.1g
Protein	4.6 g
Cholesterol	12 mg
Sodium	267 mg

* Percent Daily Values are based on a 2,000 calorie diet.

Pesto Spinach and Tomatoes

Ingredients

- 2 tbsps olive oil
- 2 garlic cloves, coarsely chopped
- 1 bunch fresh spinach, chopped
- 1 pint cherry tomatoes, halved
- 2 tbsps prepared basil pesto

Directions

- In a large skillet, heat oil on medium heat and sauté garlic for about 1 minute.
- Add spinach and stir fry for about 2 minutes or till wilted.
- Stir in tomatoes and cook for about 2 minutes.
- Stir in the pesto and serve hot.

Amount per serving (2 total)

Timing Information:

Preparation	10 m
Cooking	5 m
Total Time	15 m

Nutritional Information:

Calories	272 kcal
Fat	21.8 g
Carbohydrates	15.1g
Protein	9.1 g
Cholesterol	5 mg
Sodium	267 mg

* Percent Daily Values are based on a 2,000 calorie diet.

Roasted Cauliflower, Garlic, and Leek Soup

Ingredients

- 1 head cauliflower, cut into florets
- 3 tbsps olive oil
- salt and ground black pepper to taste
- 4 cloves garlic
- 1/4 C. butter
- 2 stalks celery
- 1 leek - split, cleaned, and minced
- 1/4 C. all-purpose flour
- 4 C. chicken broth
- 1 tsp dried marjoram

Directions

- Set your oven to 400 degrees F before doing anything else and grease a baking sheet.
- In a bowl, add cauliflower and drizzle with oil and sprinkle with salt and black pepper.
- Spread the cauliflower and garlic into the prepared baking sheet and Cook everything in the oven for about 15 minutes.
- Flip the cauliflower and garlic and sauté for about 10 minutes.
- In a large pan, melt butter on medium heat and sauté the leeks and celery for about 5 minutes or till softened.

- Stir in the flour and cook, stirring continuously for about 2-3 minutes.
- Add the broth, stirring continuously till well combined.
- Stir in the cauliflower mixture and marjoram and bring to a gentle simmer and cook for about 10 minutes.
- Remove everything from the heat and with an immersion blender, puree the soup to the desired consistency.
- Season with salt and black pepper and serve hot.

Amount per serving (4 total)

Timing Information:

Preparation	15 m
Cooking	45 m
Total Time	1 h

Nutritional Information:

Calories	292 kcal
Fat	22.5 g
Carbohydrates	19.4g
Protein	5.5 g
Cholesterol	36 mg
Sodium	1145 mg

* Percent Daily Values are based on a 2,000 calorie diet.

Chicken & Mushroom Kabobs with Rice

Ingredients

- 1/2 C. light mayonnaise
- 1 tsp minced garlic
- 1/2 tsp curry powder
- 1/2 tsp chili powder
- 1/2 tsp ground ginger
- 1 1/2 lbs skinless, boneless chicken breast halves - cubed
- 1 C. uncooked white rice
- 2 C. water
- 8 oz. fresh mushrooms, sliced
- 1 tomato, diced
- 3 green onions, chopped
- skewers

Directions

- In a large bowl, mix together the mayonnaise, garlic, ginger, chili powder and curry powder.
- Add the cubed chicken and coat it with the mixture generously and refrigerate, covered for about 2-4 hours.
- Set your grill to medium-high heat and grease the grill grate.
- Meanwhile in a pan, mix together the water and rice and bring to a boil.
- Reduce the heat to low and simmer, covered for about 20 minutes or till all the liquid is absorbed.
- Remove the chicken from the refrigerator and discard the excess marinade.
- Thread the chicken and mushrooms onto skewers.

- Cook on grill for about 5-10 minutes or till desired doneness, flipping occasionally.
- Place rice onto serving plates and top them with the skewers.
- Serve with a garnishing of tomato and onion.

Amount per serving (4 total)

Timing Information:

Preparation	15 m
Cooking	30 m
Total Time	2 h 45 m

Nutritional Information:

Calories	394 kcal
Fat	4.8 g
Carbohydrates	43.7g
Protein	41.5 g
Cholesterol	97 mg
Sodium	96 mg

* Percent Daily Values are based on a 2,000 calorie diet.

Shawarma

Ingredients

- 1 tbsp ground coriander
- 1 tbsp ground cumin
- 1 tbsp ground cardamom
- 1 tbsp chili powder
- 1 tbsp grill seasoning
- 1 tsp smoked paprika
- 1/2 tsp ground turmeric
- 1 lemon, juiced, divided
- 1 large clove garlic, minced
- 5 tbsps extra-virgin olive oil, divided
- 4 (6 oz.) skinless, boneless chicken breast halves
- 1 large onion, sliced
- 1 red bell pepper, sliced
- 1 yellow bell pepper, sliced
- salt and ground black pepper to taste
- 1 1/2 C. Greek yogurt
- 1/4 C. tahini
- 1 tsp extra-virgin olive oil
- 4 pita bread rounds

Directions

- Set your outdoor grill to high heat and grease the grill grate.
- In a large bowl, add spices, garlic, 1/2 of lemon juice and 3 tbsps of oil and mix till a paste forms.
- Add the chicken breasts and coat with paste generously.
- Cook on the grill for about 12 minutes, flipping once half way or till desired doneness.

- Place the chicken breasts onto a plate and let them cool and then cut into thin slices.
- In a large skillet, heat 2 tbsps of oil on medium heat and sauté the bell peppers and onion with salt and black pepper for about 5 minutes.
- In a bowl, mix together yogurt, tahini, remaining lemon juice, 1 tsp of oil and salt.
- Cook the pita on grill for about 1 minute per side or till lightly charred.
- Divide chicken and bell pepper mixture over pita breads evenly.
- Serve with a topping of tahini yogurt.

Amount per serving (4 total)

Timing Information:

Preparation	20 m
Cooking	20 m
Total Time	45 m

Nutritional Information:

Calories	737 kcal
Fat	39.6 g
Carbohydrates	46.4g
Protein	49.1 g
Cholesterol	114 mg
Sodium	1133 mg

* Percent Daily Values are based on a 2,000 calorie diet.

Buttered Apple Scones

Ingredients

- 2 C. all-purpose flour
- 1/4 C. white sugar
- 2 tsps baking powder
- 1/2 tsp baking soda
- 1/2 tsp salt
- 1/4 C. butter, chilled
- 1 apple - peeled, cored and shredded
- 1/2 C. milk
- 2 tbsps milk
- 2 tbsps white sugar
- 1/2 tsp ground cinnamon

Directions

- Set your oven to 425 degrees F before doing anything else and grease a large baking sheet.
- In a large bowl, mix together flour, sugar, baking soda, baking powder and salt.
- With a pastry cutter, cut the butter into the flour mixture and mix till a crumbly mixture forms.
- Add 1/2 C. of milk and apple and mix till a soft dough forms.
- Place the dough onto a floured surface and gently, knead it about 8-10 times.
- Roll the dough into 2 (6-inch) circles.
- Arrange the circles onto the prepared baking sheet.
- With remaining milk, brush the tops of the circles and sprinkle with the remaining sugar and cinnamon.

- Carefully, cut each circle into 6 equal sized wedges and cook them in the oven for about 15 minutes or till golden brown.
- Serve warm with a topping of butter.

Amount per serving (12 total)

Timing Information:

Preparation	15 m
Cooking	15 m
Total Time	30 m

Nutritional Information:

Calories	147 kcal
Fat	4.3 g
Carbohydrates	24.6g
Protein	2.6 g
Cholesterol	11 mg
Sodium	264 mg

* Percent Daily Values are based on a 2,000 calorie diet.

Moist Egg Pancakes

Ingredients

- 1 C. all-purpose flour
- 1 tbsp baking powder
- 1 C. milk
- 3 egg yolks
- 3 egg whites

Directions

- In a bowl, mix together flour and baking powder.
- Add the egg yolk and milk and mix till smooth.
- In another bowl, add the egg whites and beat till stiff peaks form.
- Gently, fold in 1/3 of beaten egg whites and then quickly, fold in the remaining egg whites.
- Lightly, grease a frying pan or griddle and heat on medium heat.
- Add about 1/4 C. of mixture on the griddle and cook till golden brown from both sides.

Amount per serving (4 total)

Timing Information:

Preparation	10 m
Cooking	10 m
Total Time	20 m

Nutritional Information:

Calories	197 kcal
Fat	4.8 g
Carbohydrates	28g
Protein	9.9 g
Cholesterol	159 mg
Sodium	325 mg

* Percent Daily Values are based on a 2,000 calorie diet.

Tangy Swordfish

Ingredients

- 4 cloves garlic
- 1/3 C. white wine
- 1/4 C. lemon juice
- 2 tbsps soy sauce
- 2 tbsps olive oil
- 1 tbsp poultry seasoning
- 1/4 tsp salt
- 1/8 tsp pepper
- 4 swordfish steaks
- 1 tbsp chopped fresh parsley
- 4 slices lemon, for garnish

Directions

- In a large glass baking dish, mix together all the ingredients except the steaks, parsley and lemon slices.
- Add the swordfish sticks and coat it with the mixture generously and refrigerate for at least 1 hour, stirring occasionally.
- Set your outdoor grill to high heat and grease the grill grate.
- Cook on the grill for about 10-12 minutes, flipping once half way.
- Serve with a garnishing of parsley and lemon wedges.

Amount per serving (4 total)

Timing Information:

Preparation	10 m
Cooking	12 m
Total Time	22 m

Nutritional Information:

Calories	258 kcal
Fat	12.3 g
Carbohydrates	5.6g
Protein	27.6 g
Cholesterol	52 mg
Sodium	708 mg

* Percent Daily Values are based on a 2,000 calorie diet.

Herbed Cheesy Sandwich

Ingredients

- 1 tbsp butter, softened
- 2 slices bread
- 2 slices sharp Cheddar cheese
- 1 tbsp chopped parsley
- 1 tsp chopped basil
- 1 tsp oregano
- 1 tsp chopped fresh rosemary
- 1 tsp chopped fresh dill

Directions

- Place butter over each slice on one side evenly and place the cheddar slices over the unbuttered side of 1 slice.
- Place the herb mixture over the unbuttered side of the remaining slice.
- Make a sandwich by placing the buttered sides outwards.
- Heat a nonstick skillet on medium heat and cook the sandwich for about 3 minutes per side.

Amount per serving (1 total)

Timing Information:

Preparation	10 m
Cooking	6 m
Total Time	16 m

Nutritional Information:

Calories	470 kcal
Fat	32.2 g
Carbohydrates	27.4g
Protein	18.4 g
Cholesterol	90 mg
Sodium	777 mg

* Percent Daily Values are based on a 2,000 calorie diet.

Sweet & Sour Pork with Bell Peppers

Ingredients

Marinade:

- 1/4 C. rice wine vinegar
- 2 tbsps minced garlic
- 1 tbsp brown sugar
- 5 tbsps olive oil
- salt and pepper to taste

Stir Fry:

- 4 boneless pork loin chops, cut into bite sized pieces
- 5 tbsps vegetable oil
- 3 tbsps finely chopped fresh ginger root
- 1 tbsp hot chile paste
- 5 tbsps teriyaki sauce
- 1 green bell pepper, cut into strips
- 1 red bell pepper, cut into strips
- 1 yellow bell pepper, cut into strips
- salt and pepper to taste
- 1/4 C. blanched slivered almonds
- 2 tbsps chopped fresh mint

Directions

- In a large bowl, add the garlic, vinegar, olive oil, brown sugar, salt and black pepper and mix till well combined.
- Add the pork and coat it with the mixture generously and keep aside at room temperature for about 30 minutes.

- Heat a large nonstick skillet on medium heat and toast the almonds till fragrant and golden brown.
- Transfer the almonds into a bowl.
- In the same skillet, heat the vegetable oil on medium-high heat.
- Remove the pork from the bowl and discard the marinade.
- In the skillet, stir in the pork, chile paste and ginger.
- Increase the heat to high and stir in the teriyaki sauce and cook, stirring continuously till the pork becomes white.
- Add bell peppers and cook, stirring continuously till desired doneness.
- Serve with a garnishing of mint and toasted almonds.

Amount per serving (4 total)

Timing Information:

Preparation	30 m
Cooking	10 m
Total Time	1 h 10 m

Nutritional Information:

Calories	579 kcal
Fat	45.1 g
Carbohydrates	17.5g
Protein	27.5 g
Cholesterol	59 mg
Sodium	935 mg

* Percent Daily Values are based on a 2,000 calorie diet.

Bacon Wrapped Partridge Breasts

Ingredients

- 4 boneless partridge breast halves
- 8 slices bacon, optional
- 1 C. chicken broth
- toothpicks
- 1 C. white wine
- 2 shallots, chopped
- 4 cloves garlic, chopped
- 1 tsp salt
- freshly ground black pepper to taste
- 3 tbsps all-purpose flour

Directions

- Set your oven to 325 degrees F before doing anything else.
- Heat a large nonstick skillet on medium-high heat and cook the bacon till it releases its juices.
- Transfer the bacon into a bowl.
- In the same skillet, add the breast halves and cook for about 2 minutes per side.
- Transfer the breasts onto a plate and wrap each with 2 bacon slices and secure with toothpicks.
- Place the pan drippings into a baking dish to cover the bottom.
- Arrange the wrapped breast halves into the baking dish in a single layer followed by the wine, broth, garlic, shallot, salt and black pepper.
- Cook everything in the oven for about 45 minutes.

- In a pan, add the drippings from the baking dish and mix with flour on medium-low heat.
- Cook, stirring continuously till the gravy becomes thick.
- Serve the breasts with gravy.

Amount per serving (4 total)

Timing Information:

Preparation	25 m
Cooking	1 h
Total Time	1 h 25 m

Nutritional Information:

Calories	484 kcal
Fat	26 g
Carbohydrates	12.1g
Protein	30 g
Cholesterol	112 mg
Sodium	1331 mg

* Percent Daily Values are based on a 2,000 calorie diet.

Potato Fries with Gravy

Ingredients

- 1 quart vegetable oil for frying
- 1 (10.25 oz.) can beef gravy
- 5 medium potatoes, cut into fries
- 2 C. cheese curds

Directions

- In a deep heavy skillet or deep fryer, heat the oil to 365 degrees F.
- Meanwhile in a pan, heat the gravy.
- In the hot oil, fry the potatoes fries in batches for about 5 minutes or till golden brown.
- Transfer the fries onto paper towel lined plate.
- In serving plates, place fries and top with cheese curds.
- Serve immediately with a topping of warm gravy.

Amount per serving (4 total)

Timing Information:

Preparation	5 m
Cooking	20 m
Total Time	25 m

Nutritional Information:

Calories	708 kcal
Fat	46.3 g
Carbohydrates	51g
Protein	23.8 g
Cholesterol	78 mg
Sodium	773 mg

* Percent Daily Values are based on a 2,000 calorie diet.

Cabbage Rolls in Tomato Gravy

Ingredients

- 2 C. uncooked long-grain rice, washed
- 4 C. water
- 2 large heads savoy cabbage
- 1 C. water
- 2 onions, chopped
- 3 tbsps butter
- 3/4 C. uncooked long-grain rice
- 1 lb extra-lean ground beef
- 1/2 lb pork sausage
- 4 cloves garlic, minced
- 2 tsps dried dill weed
- 3/4 tsp salt
- 1/2 tsp ground black pepper
- 1/2 tsp white sugar
- 1 (26 oz.) can condensed tomato soup
- 1 (28 oz.) can whole peeled tomatoes, with liquid
- 8 bay leaves

Directions

- Set your oven to 350 degrees F before doing anything else and grease a 9x5-inch baking dish.
- In a pan mix together 2 C. rice and 4 C. of water and bring to a boil.
- Reduce the heat and simmer, covered for about 20 minutes or till all the liquid is absorbed.
- Meanwhile core the cabbage heads and in a microwave safe bowl, place 1 head cabbage, core side down and 1/2 C. of water.

- Cover the bowl and microwave on High for about 20 minutes, flipping once half way.
- Repeat with the remaining cabbage head.
- Remove everything from the microwave and let them cool completely.
- Carefully, separate the leaves from both cabbage heads, removing the tough ribs.
- In a skillet, melt 3 tbsp of butter and sauté half of the onion till just tender.
- Transfer the cooked onion into a large bowl.
- Add the remaining uncooked onion, uncooked and cooked rice, pork sausage, dill weed, garlic, sugar, salt and black pepper and mix till well combined.
- Place about 2 tbsps of meat mixture over each cabbage leaf.
- Carefully, roll the leaves around the filling and tuck the ends.
- Arrange some extra cabbage leaves in the bottom of 2 (13x9-inch) casserole dishes.
- Place the rolls over the leaves in a single layer.
- In a food processor, add tomatoes and soup and pulse till a smooth puree forms.
- Cover the rolls of both dishes with tomato mixture.
- With foil cover the dishes tightly and Cook everything in the oven for about 2 hours.
- Remove the dish from the oven and keep them aside for about 15 minutes.
- Uncover the casserole dishes and serve hot.

Amount per serving (12 total)

Timing Information:

Preparation	30 m
Cooking	2 h
Total Time	2 h 30 m

Nutritional Information:

Calories	441 kcal
Fat	16 g
Carbohydrates	59.5g
Protein	18 g
Cholesterol	43 mg
Sodium	801 mg

* Percent Daily Values are based on a 2,000 calorie diet.

Coconut & Raisin Tart

Ingredients

- 2 C. all-purpose flour
- 1 C. shortening
- 1/2 tsp salt
- 5 tbsps ice water
- 1 C. packed brown sugar
- 1 egg
- 1/2 tbsp butter
- 1/2 tsp vanilla extract
- 1 tbsp hot water
- 1/2 C. flaked coconut
- 1/2 C. chopped walnuts
- 1/2 C. raisins

Directions

- Set your oven to 350 degrees F before doing anything else and grease a muffin or tart pan.
- In a large bowl, sift together flour and salt.
- With a pastry cutter, cut the shortening into the flour mixture and add 1 tbsp of chilled water and mix till a dough forms.
- Shape the dough into a ball and cover with plastic wrap and refrigerate for at least 15 minutes.
- Place the dough between 2 wax paper sheets and roll completely.
- Cut the dough into 12 shells and place into prepared muffin or tart pan.
- Meanwhile in a baking pan, place the coconut and walnuts and Cook everything in the oven for about 5-10 minutes or till toasted.
- Now, increase the temperature of the oven to 450 degrees F.

- Place the raisins in the bottom of the tart shells evenly.
- In a bowl, add the butter, egg, sugar, vanilla and hot water and beat till well combined and fold in toasted coconut and walnuts.
- Transfer the mixture into the tart shells evenly and Cook everything in the oven for about 10-12 minutes or till golden brown.

Amount per serving (12 total)

Timing Information:

Preparation	15 min
Cooking	10 min
Total Time	25 min

Nutritional Information:

Calories	371 kcal
Fat	22.3 g
Carbohydrates	41g
Protein	3.7 g
Cholesterol	17 mg
Sodium	121 mg

* Percent Daily Values are based on a 2,000 calorie diet.

Nova Scotia Quiche

Ingredients

- 1 C. all-purpose baking mix
- 1/4 tsp salt
- 1/4 tsp ground black pepper
- 1/3 C. milk
- 3 slices turkey bacon, chopped
- 1 small onion, chopped
- 2 C. shredded Cheddar cheese
- 4 eggs
- 1 tsp salt
- 1/4 tsp hot pepper sauce
- 1 (12 fluid oz.) can evaporated milk, heated

Directions

- Set your oven to 400 degrees F before doing anything else and grease a 9-inch pie dish.
- Mix together the baking mix, salt and black pepper in a bowl.
- Slowly, add the milk and mix till well combined and moistened.
- Place the mixture onto a floured surface and knead till a dough forms.
- With a rolling pin, roll the dough into a 12-inch round.
- Transfer the dough into prepared pie pan and with your hands, press gently and then fold the edges.
- Heat a large deep skillet on medium-high heat and cook bacon and onion till bacon is browned.
- Drain the bacon and then crumble it.

- Place the bacon and the onion mixture into the pie pan, followed by the cheese.
- In a bowl, add the eggs, hot sauce and salt and beat till well combined and then mix in the hot evaporated milk.
- Place the egg mixture over the cheese evenly and Cook everything in the oven for about 5 minutes.
- Now, set the oven to 350 degrees F and cook for about 25 minutes or till set.

Amount per serving (8 total)

Timing Information:

Preparation	20 m
Cooking	40 m
Total Time	1 h

Nutritional Information:

Calories	302 kcal
Fat	19.4 g
Carbohydrates	15.9g
Protein	16.2 g
Cholesterol	141 mg
Sodium	898 mg

* Percent Daily Values are based on a 2,000 calorie diet.

Moist Corn Fritters

Ingredients

- 2 C. all-purpose flour
- 2 tsps baking powder
- 1 tsp salt
- 1/2 tsp ground black pepper
- 1 egg, beaten
- 1/2 C. milk
- 1 (15.25 oz.) can whole kernel corn
- 1 (14.75 oz.) can cream-style corn
- 1 tsp lard

Directions

- In a bowl, mix together the flour, baking powder, salt and black pepper.
- In the center of the flour mixture, make a well and add the remaining ingredients except lard and mix till well combined.
- In a skillet, heat the lard on medium-high heat.
- With a tbsp, add the corn mixture and cook for about 2-3 minutes per side or till golden brown.

Amount per serving (6 total)

Timing Information:

Preparation	15 m
Cooking	15 m
Total Time	30 m

Nutritional Information:

Calories	288 kcal
Fat	3.3 g
Carbohydrates	59.1g
Protein	9.1 g
Cholesterol	33 mg
Sodium	937 mg

* Percent Daily Values are based on a 2,000 calorie diet.

Garlicky & Lemony Mayo

Ingredients

- 3/4 C. mayonnaise
- 3 cloves garlic, minced
- 2 1/2 tbsps lemon juice
- 3/4 tsp salt
- 1/2 tsp ground black pepper

Directions

- In a small bowl, mix together all the ingredients and refrigerate, covered for at least 30 minutes.

Amount per serving (8 total)

Timing Information:

Preparation	10 m
Cooking	40 m
Total Time	50 m

Nutritional Information:

Calories	151 kcal
Fat	16.4 g
Carbohydrates	1.5g
Protein	0.3 g
Cholesterol	8 mg
Sodium	335 mg

* Percent Daily Values are based on a 2,000 calorie diet.

BEER & SPICES BRAISED SHRIMP

Ingredients

- 1 tsp garlic powder
- 1 tsp onion powder
- 1 tsp dried basil
- 1/2 tsp dried thyme
- 1/2 tsp dried rosemary
- 1/4 tsp cayenne pepper
- 1/3 tsp paprika
- 1/2 C. butter
- 4 cloves garlic, minced
- 1/4 C. beer, room temperature, optional
- 1 tbsp Worcestershire sauce
- 1 lb medium shrimp - peeled and deveined
- salt to taste

Directions

- In a small bowl, mix together the herbs and spices.
- In a large skillet, melt the butter on medium heat and sauté the garlic for about 1 minute
- Stir in the shrimp and cook for about 2 minutes.
- Stir in the spice mixture and cook for few minutes more.
- Stir in the Worcestershire sauce and beer and cook for about 1 minute or till the desired doneness.
- Season with the salt and serve.

Amount per serving (4 total)

Timing Information:

Preparation	10 m
Cooking	10 m
Total Time	20 m

Nutritional Information:

Calories	345 kcal
Fat	25.1 g
Carbohydrates	4.8g
Protein	23.8 g
Cholesterol	234 mg
Sodium	375 mg

* Percent Daily Values are based on a 2,000 calorie diet.

Tangy Prawns

Ingredients

- 1/2 C. olive oil
- 1 tbsp Dijon mustard
- 3 cloves garlic, minced
- 1 lemon, juiced
- 1 orange, juiced
- 1 tsp dried basil
- 2 tbsps white wine
- 30 tiger prawns, peeled and deveined

Directions

- In a glass baking dish, mix together all the ingredients except prawns.
- Add the prawns and coat with the mixture generously and refrigerate, covered for about 1 hour.
- Set your grill to high heat and grease the grill grate.
- Thread the prawns onto skewers and cook on the grill for about 3-5 minutes, flipping once half way.

Amount per serving (6 total)

Timing Information:

Preparation	5 m
Cooking	3 m
Total Time	8 m

Nutritional Information:

Calories	231 kcal
Fat	18.6 g
Carbohydrates	6.4g
Protein	10.2 g
Cholesterol	89 mg
Sodium	166 mg

* Percent Daily Values are based on a 2,000 calorie diet.

Canadian BBQ Sauce

Ingredients

- 1/2 C. applesauce
- 1/2 C. ketchup
- 2 C. packed brown sugar
- 6 tbsps lemon juice
- 1/2 tsp salt
- 1/2 tsp black pepper
- 1/2 tsp paprika
- 1/2 tsp garlic salt
- 1/2 tsp ground cinnamon

Directions

- In a bowl, mix together the all the ingredients.
- This sauce is best to marinate ribs for at least 30 minutes or you can also use to baste ribs during cooking.

Amount per serving (8 total)

Timing Information:

Preparation	10 m
Cooking	40 m
Total Time	50 m

Nutritional Information:

Calories	163 kcal
Fat	0.1 g
Carbohydrates	42.3g
Protein	0.4 g
Cholesterol	0 mg
Sodium	436 mg

* Percent Daily Values are based on a 2,000 calorie diet.

Baked Pollock with Veggies

Ingredients

- 2 (6 oz.) fillets pollock fillets
- 1/2 tsp paprika
- 1/2 tsp black pepper
- 1 small yellow onion, sliced
- 1 small green bell pepper, cut into strips
- 4 (1/4 inch thick) slices red tomato
- 4 slices Cheddar cheese

Directions

- Set your oven to 350 degrees F before doing anything else and grease a large casserole dish with some melted butter.
- Sprinkle the pollock fillets with black pepper and paprika evenly.
- Arrange the fillets onto the prepared baking sheet in a single layer and top with the onion, bell pepper and tomato in layers.
- Cook everything in the oven for about 15 minutes or till the desired doneness.
- Turn the oven off and top the each fillet with the 2 cheese slices and keep it in the oven for about 3 minutes or till the cheese melts.

Amount per serving (2 total)

Timing Information:

Preparation	15 m
Cooking	25 m
Total Time	40 m

Nutritional Information:

Calories	398 kcal
Fat	20.4 g
Carbohydrates	7.9g
Protein	44.5 g
Cholesterol	180 mg
Sodium	525 mg

* Percent Daily Values are based on a 2,000 calorie diet.

Easy Canadian Cookbook

Chicken & Sliders in Broth Gravy

Ingredients

- 3 lbs whole chicken
- 2 onions, quartered
- 3 stalks celery, cut into 1 inch pieces
- 2 bay leaves
- salt and pepper to taste
- 1 egg
- 4 C. all-purpose flour

Directions

- In a large pan of water, add the chicken, celery, onion, bay leaves, salt and black pepper and bring to a boil.
- Reduce the heat to low and simmer for about 2 hours or till the chicken becomes tender.
- Transfer the chicken onto a plate and let it cool.
- Meanwhile, strain the broth and discard the vegetables and bay leaves.
- After cooling, remove the meat from the bones and then chop it.
- For the sliders in a bowl, add some broth and egg and beat well.
- In a bowl, add the flour, egg mixture and the required amount of broth and mix till a dough forms.
- With your hands, knead the dough for a few minutes.
- Place the dough onto a floured surface and roll it.
- With a knife, cut the dough into 3-inch long and 1 1/2-inch wide strips.

- In a pan, add the remaining broth and bring to a boil and cook the noodles for about 5 minutes.
- Stir in the chicken and simmer till the desired thickness of the gravy. (If you like than use a little flour for the thickness of gravy)
- Stir in the salt and black pepper and serve.

Amount per serving (6 total)

Timing Information:

Preparation	30 m
Cooking	2 h 30 m
Total Time	3 h

Nutritional Information:

Calories	613 kcal
Fat	17.8 g
Carbohydrates	67.8g
Protein	41.8 g
Cholesterol	131 mg
Sodium	239 mg

* Percent Daily Values are based on a 2,000 calorie diet.

Raisin Pudding

Ingredients

- 1 C. all-purpose flour
- 1/3 C. white sugar
- 1 tsp baking powder
- 1/2 C. raisins
- 1/2 C. milk
- 1 C. packed brown sugar
- 2 C. boiling water
- 1 tbsp butter
- 1 tsp vanilla extract

Directions

- Set your oven to 350 degrees F before doing anything else and grease a large casserole dish with some melted butter.
- In a bowl, sift together the flour, white sugar and baking powder.
- Add the milk and raisins and stir to combine well.
- Transfer the mixture into the prepared casserole dish evenly.
- In a bowl, mix together the remaining ingredients and place the mixture over the flour mixture evenly.
- Cook everything in the oven for about 30 minutes and serve warm.

Amount per serving (10 total)

Timing Information:

Preparation	15 min
Cooking	15 min
Total Time	30 min

Nutritional Information:

Calories	194 kcal
Fat	1.5 g
Carbohydrates	44.3g
Protein	2 g
Cholesterol	4 mg
Sodium	71 mg

* Percent Daily Values are based on a 2,000 calorie diet.

Mushroom Pastries

Ingredients

- cooking spray
- 3 green onions
- 1 (10 oz.) can mushroom pieces, drained
- 2 tbsps butter
- 2 tbsps cornstarch
- 1/2 C. half-and-half
- salt and ground black pepper to taste
- 1 pinch garlic powder
- 10 slices sandwich bread

Directions

- Set your oven to 350 degrees F before doing anything else and grease a baking sheet. With a sharp knife, mince the mushrooms and green onion finely.
- In a pan, melt the butter on medium heat and sauté the mushroom and green onion for about 2 minutes or till fragrant. Meanwhile in a bowl, mix together the half-and-half and cornstarch and slowly, add in pan, stirring continuously.
- Cook, stirring occasionally for about 3 minutes or till the mixture becomes thick. Stir in the salt and black pepper and remove from heat.
- With a rolling pin, roll the bread slices till thin.
- Divide the mushroom mixture over each slice evenly and then roll tightly.
- Carefully, cut each roll into 1-inch thick rounds.
- Arrange the slices into the prepared baking sheet in a single layer and Cook everything in the oven for about 10 minutes or till golden brown.

Amount per serving (10 total)

Timing Information:

Preparation	20 m
Cooking	15 m
Total Time	35 m

Nutritional Information:

Calories	118 kcal
Fat	4.6 g
Carbohydrates	16.5g
Protein	2.9 g
Cholesterol	11 mg
Sodium	328 mg

* Percent Daily Values are based on a 2,000 calorie diet.

CRISPY SMELTS

Ingredients

- 1 C. all-purpose flour
- 2 tbsps salt
- 3/4 lb cleaned smelt
- 1 C. vegetable oil for frying

Directions

- In a deep frying pan, add the oil on medium heat and cook till hot.
- In a shallow dish, mix together the flour and salt and coat the smelt with the flour mixture evenly.
- Fry the smelt for about 2-3 minutes per side or till crispy.
- Transfer the smelt onto a paper towel lined plate to drain.

Amount per serving (3 total)

Timing Information:

Preparation	10 m
Cooking	10 m
Total Time	20 m

Nutritional Information:

Calories	440 kcal
Fat	19 g
Carbohydrates	43.1g
Protein	22.4 g
Cholesterol	91 mg
Sodium	4845 mg

* Percent Daily Values are based on a 2,000 calorie diet.

Simple Shepherd's Pie

Ingredients

- 5 potatoes, peeled and cubed
- 1/2 C. margarine, divided
- 1/3 C. milk
- salt and ground black pepper to taste
- 2 onions, minced
- 1 1/4 lbs ground beef
- 1 (11 oz.) can whole kernel corn, drained
- 1 (14.75 oz.) can cream-style corn

Directions

- Set your oven to 350 degrees F before doing anything else and lightly grease a 13x9-inch casserole dish.
- In a large pan of salted water, add the potatoes and bring to a boil and reduce the heat to low.
- Simmer for about 20 minutes or till tender and drain well.
- Transfer the potatoes into a bowl, with 2 tbsps of the margarine, milk, salt and black pepper and mash till well combined.
- In a large skillet, melt 2 tbsps of the margarine on medium heat and sauté the onion for about 5 minutes or till tender.
- Transfer the onion into prepared casserole dish evenly.
- In the same skillet, add the beef and cook for about 5 minutes and transfer over onion evenly.

- With a paper towel, wipe out the skillet and add the corn and creamed corn on medium heat.
- Cook, stirring occasionally for about 5 minutes or till bubbly.
- Place the corn mixture over beef evenly, followed by the mashed potatoes.
- Place the remaining butter on top in the shape of dots and sprinkle with the salt and black pepper.
- Cook everything in the oven for about 30 minutes or till the top becomes golden brown.

Amount per serving (8 total)

Timing Information:

Preparation	30 m
Cooking	45 m
Total Time	1 h 15 m

Nutritional Information:

Calories	437 kcal
Fat	23.2 g
Carbohydrates	43g
Protein	17.1 g
Cholesterol	44 mg
Sodium	496 mg

* Percent Daily Values are based on a 2,000 calorie diet.

Cheesy Smoked Meat Tortilla

Ingredients

- 1 (12 inch) flour tortilla
- 2 tbsps mayonnaise
- 1 tbsp prepared yellow mustard
- 2 oz. thinly sliced Montreal smoked meat
- 1/4 C. shredded Mexican cheese blend
- 1/4 C. vegetable oil for frying

Directions

- In a microwave, warm the tortillas on high for about 20 seconds or till soft.
- In a bowl, mix together the mustard and mayonnaise.
- Place the mayo mixture in the center of the tortilla, leaving 1-inch edges.
- Place the smoked meat over the mayo mixture and top with the cheese blend.
- Fold the bottom and sides of the tortilla.
- In a skillet, heat oil on medium heat and place the wrap, seam side down.
- Cook for about 2 minutes per side, pressing gently with the back of a spatula.
- Cut in half and serve.

Amount per serving (1 total)

Timing Information:

Preparation	5 m
Cooking	5 m
Total Time	10 m

Nutritional Information:

Calories	839 kcal
Fat	54.9 g
Carbohydrates	62.9g
Protein	23.8 g
Cholesterol	65 mg
Sodium	1349 mg

* Percent Daily Values are based on a 2,000 calorie diet.

Creamy Lobster Sandwich

Ingredients

- 1/2 C. butter
- 2 C. cooked lobster meat
- 1 tsp salt
- 1/4 tsp ground black pepper
- 1 tbsp cornstarch
- 2 C. light cream, divided
- 8 slices bread
- 2 tbsps butter

Directions

- In a large frying pan, melt the butter on medium-low heat and cook the lobster for about 5 minutes or till heated completely.
- Meanwhile in a bowl, add the cornstarch and 1 tbsp of the cream and beat till well combined.
- Stir in the remaining cream, salt and black pepper.
- Slowly, add the cornstarch mixture, stirring continuously.
- Cook, stirring continuously for about 5 minutes or till the sauce becomes thick.
- Spread the remaining butter over each toasted bread slice.
- Place the lobster mixture over 4 bread slices and top with the remaining slices to make a sandwich.
- Spread the remaining lobster mixture on the top of each sandwich and serve.

Amount per serving (4 total)

Timing Information:

Preparation	10 m
Cooking	15 m
Total Time	25 m

Nutritional Information:

Calories	700 kcal
Fat	51.5 g
Carbohydrates	31.7g
Protein	28 g
Cholesterol	222 mg
Sodium	1341 mg

* Percent Daily Values are based on a 2,000 calorie diet.

Spiced Meatballs Stew

Ingredients

- 3/4 C. all-purpose flour
- 2 tbsps butter
- 1 large onion, minced
- 1 tsp ground cinnamon
- 1 tsp ground nutmeg
- 1 tsp ground cloves
- 2 lbs ground pork
- 2 tbsps dried parsley
- 1 egg
- 1/2 C. dry bread crumbs
- 6 C. reduced sodium chicken broth
- 1 bay leaf
- 1/4 C. cold water
- salt and ground black pepper to taste
- 4 potatoes, peeled and cubed

Directions

- Set your oven to 425 degrees F before doing anything else.
- In a large baking sheet, spread the flour in a thin layer and Cook everything in the oven for about 10-15 minutes or till browned lightly, stirring occasionally.
- Remove from the oven and transfer into a shallow dish.
- In a large pan, melt the butter on medium heat and sauté onion for about 5 minutes.
- Transfer the onion into a large bowl and let it cool.
- In the bowl of onion, add the pork, breadcrumbs, egg, parsley and spices and mix till well combined.

- Make 1-inch sized balls from the mixture and roll the balls into toasted flour evenly.
- Reserve the remaining flour in a bowl.
- In the same pan, add the broth and bay leaf on medium heat and bring to a boil.
- Carefully, add the meatballs into the pan and simmer for about 20 minutes.
- Add the potatoes and simmer for about 20 minutes further.
- With a slotted spoon, transfer the meatballs into a bowl and discard the bay leaf.
- In the bowl of flour, add the water and mix till well combined.
- Slowly, add the flour mixture in the pan, stirring continuously and bring to a boil.
- Cook, stirring continuously for about 5 minutes or till the gravy becomes thick.
- Carefully add the meatballs in the gravy and season with salt and black pepper.
- Serve hot.

Amount per serving (8 total)

Timing Information:

Preparation	30 m
Cooking	1 h
Total Time	1 h 30 m

Nutritional Information:

Calories	445 kcal
Fat	20.9 g
Carbohydrates	35.6g
Protein	27.9 g
Cholesterol	107 mg
Sodium	230 mg

* Percent Daily Values are based on a 2,000 calorie diet.

CHEESY SPAGHETTI

Ingredients

- 1 lb spaghetti
- 1 tbsp olive oil
- 8 slices bacon, diced
- 1 tbsp olive oil
- 1 onion, chopped
- 1 clove garlic, minced
- 1/4 C. dry white wine
- 4 eggs
- 1/2 C. grated Parmesan cheese
- pinch of salt and black pepper
- 2 tbsps chopped fresh parsley
- 2 tbsps grated Parmesan cheese

Directions

- In a large pan of lightly salted boiling water, add the spaghetti and cook the spaghetti till desired doneness and drain well.
- In a bowl, add the spaghetti and 1 tbsp of the oil and toss to coat well and keep aside.
- Meanwhile heat a large skillet and cook the bacon till crisp.
- Transfer the bacon onto a paper towel lined plate, leaving 2 tbsps of fat in the skillet.
- In the same skillet, heat the remaining 1 tbsp of the oil with bacon fat on medium heat and sauté the onion till tender.
- Stir in the garlic and sauté for about 1 minute.
- Stir in the wine and cook for 1 minute further.
- Stir in the cooked spaghetti and bacon and toss till heated completely.

- Stir in the eggs and cook, tossing continuously till the eggs set.
- Stir in 1/2 C. of the cheese till well combined.
- Stir in the salt and black pepper and remove from heat.
- Serve immediately with a garnishing of the remaining cheese and parsley.

Amount per serving (8 total)

Timing Information:

Preparation	20 m
Cooking	20 m
Total Time	40 m

Nutritional Information:

Calories	444 kcal
Fat	21.1 g
Carbohydrates	44.7g
Protein	16.4 g
Cholesterol	118 mg
Sodium	369 mg

* Percent Daily Values are based on a 2,000 calorie diet.

Cheesy Lobster in Creamy Sauce

Ingredients

- 1 (1 1/2 lb) cooked lobster
- 2 tbsps butter
- 1 shallot, finely chopped
- 1 3/8 C. fresh fish stock 300ml
- 1/4 C. white wine 50ml
- 1/4 C. double cream 50ml
- 1/2 tsp hot English mustard
- 1 tbsp fresh lemon juice
- 2 tbsps chopped fresh parsley
- salt and freshly ground black pepper to taste
- 1/4 C. freshly grated Parmesan cheese 50ml

Directions

- Set the broiler of your oven.
- With a sharp knife, half the lobster lengthwise and remove the meat from the tail and claws.
- Now, remove the meat from the head and then chop the meat and transfer into the shell again.
- Arrange the lobster into a broiler pan.
- In a large skillet, melt the butter on medium heat and sauté the shallot till tender.
- Stir in the cream, wine and broth and bring to a boil and cook till the mixture reduces to half.

- Stir in the remaining ingredients except cheese and pour over lobster halves in a broiler pan.
- Top the cheese evenly and cook under the broiler for about 3-4 minutes or till golden brown.
- Serve immediately.

Amount per serving (2 total)

Timing Information:

Preparation	30 m
Cooking	10 m
Total Time	40 m

Nutritional Information:

Calories	653 kcal
Fat	28 g
Carbohydrates	13.5g
Protein	76.7 g
Cholesterol	1323 mg
Sodium	12253 mg

* Percent Daily Values are based on a 2,000 calorie diet.

Delicious Apple Crisp

Ingredients

- 5 -6 tart apples, peeled, cored and sliced
- 2 tbsp sugar
- 2 tbsp lightly packed brown sugar
- 1 1/2 tsp cinnamon
- 2 tbsp butter, melted
- Topping
- 3/4 C. flour, plus
- 2 tbsp flour
- 6 tbsp oatmeal
- 7 tbsp sugar
- 7 tbsp lightly packed brown sugar
- 12 tbsp butter, cut in small pieces

Directions

- Set your oven to 375 degrees F before doing anything.
- In a casserole dish, add the apples, cinnamon and both sugars and stir to combine.
- Keep aside for about 20 minutes.
- Place the melted butter over the apple slices evenly.
- For the topping in a bowl, mix together the oatmeal, flour and both sugars.
- Add the chopped butter and mix till a coarse crumb forms.
- Place the crumb mixture over apple slices and cook in the oven for about 30-40 minutes.
- Serve warm.

Amount per serving: 6

Timing Information:

Preparation	25 mins
Total Time	1 hr 5 mins

Nutritional Information:

Calories	555.0
Fat	27.6g
Cholesterol	71.2mg
Sodium	244.8mg
Carbohydrates	77.9g
Protein	3.2g

* Percent Daily Values are based on a 2,000 calorie diet.

Meat Pie in Quebec Style

Ingredients

- 1 1/2 pounds ground pork
- 1 large baking potato
- 1 large onion, minced
- 1/2 teaspoon salt
- 1/2 teaspoon ground black pepper
- 1/2 teaspoon ground cinnamon
- 1/4 teaspoon ground cloves
- 1 dash ground allspice
- 1/2 cup water
- 1 recipe pastry for a 9 inch double crust deep dish pie
- 1 egg
- 1/4 teaspoon paprika

Directions

- Set your oven to 400 degrees F before doing anything else.
- Cook the potatoes in the oven for about 30-45 minutes.
- Remove from the oven and cool slightly.
- Peel the potatoes and mash completely.
- In a large skillet, simmer the pork, mashed potatoes, onion and spices for about 1 hour.
- Now, set your oven to 350 degrees F.
- Meanwhile, arrange the pastry in a deep pie dish.
- Place the pork filling over the crust evenly.
- Cover the filling with the top crust.
- With your fingers, pinch the edges to seal the filling.

- Coat the crust with the beaten egg and sprinkle with the paprika.
- Cut slits in top crust so steam can escape.
- Cook in the oven for about 50 minutes.

Amount per serving: 8

Timing Information:

| Preparation | 40 mins |
| Total Time | 2 hr 35 mins |

Nutritional Information:

Calories	485
Fat	32g
Cholesterol	85mg
Sodium	565mg
Carbohydrates	30g
Protein	17.9g

* Percent Daily Values are based on a 2,000 calorie diet.

Quebec Cheesy French Fries

Ingredients

- French fries
- gravy
- cheese (usually mozza)

Directions

- In a large microwave safe dish, place the French fries and top with the cheese and gravy.
- Microwave on high till cheese melts completely.
- Serve with a garnishin of the green onion.

Amount per serving: 2

Timing Information:

Preparation	5 mins
Total Time	15 mins

Nutritional Information:

Calories	1.0
Fat	5.0g
Cholesterol	7.0mg
Sodium	5.0mg
Carbohydrates	7.0g
Protein	6.0g

* Percent Daily Values are based on a 2,000 calorie diet.

British Columbian Dessert

Ingredients

BOTTOM LAYER

- 1/2 C. butter, softened
- 1/4 C. granulated sugar
- 5 tbsp cocoa
- 1 large egg, beaten
- 1 3/4 C. graham cracker crumbs
- 1/2 C. finely chopped walnuts
- 1 C. fine coconut

MIDDLE LAYER

- 1/2 C. butter
- 3 tbsp milk
- 2 tbsp vanilla custard powder
- 2 C. icing sugar
- TOPPING
- 2/3 C. semi-sweet chocolate chips
- 4 tbsp butter

Directions

- For the bottom layer in a double layer, melt the butter, cocoa powder and granulated sugar.
- Add the egg and cook, stirring continuously till mixture becomes thick.
- Remove from the heat and immediately, stir in the remaining ingredients.
- Transfer the mixture into a 9x9-inch baking dish and with your hands, press down the mixture firmly.
- For the middle layer in a bowl, add all the ingredients and beat till light.
- Place the mixture over the bottom layer evenly.

- For the topping in a pan, melt together the chocolate chips and butter on low heat.
- Remove from the heat and keep aside to cool.
- Place the cooled but runny chocolate mixture over the middle layer evenly.
- Refrigerate to chill completely.
- With a sharp knife, cut the mixture into desired size squares and serve.

Amount per serving: 1

Timing Information:

Preparation	15 mins
Total Time	30 mins

Nutritional Information:

Calories	151.8
Fat	10.5g
Cholesterol	22.2mg
Sodium	79.7mg
Carbohydrates	14.4g
Protein	1.2g

* Percent Daily Values are based on a 2,000 calorie diet.

Classic Canadian Fried Pastries

Ingredients

- 1/2 C. warm water
- 5 tsp dry yeast
- 1 pinch sugar
- 1 C. warm milk
- 1/3 C. sugar
- 1 1/2 tsp salt
- 1 tsp vanilla
- 2 eggs
- 1/3 C. oil
- 4 1/4-5 C. unbleached all-purpose flour
- oil (for frying)
- granulated sugar (for dusting)
- cinnamon

Directions

- In a large bowl, mix together the warm water, yeast and pinch of sugar.
- Keep aside for some time till the yeast dissolves completely.
- Add most of the flour, remaining sugar, eggs, milk, 1/3 C. of the oil, vanilla and milk and mix till a soft dough forms.
- Knead the dough for about 5-8 minutes, adding required amount of the flour.
- In a large greased bowl, place the dough and refrigerate, covered for about 30-40 minutes.
- Remove from the refrigerator and keep in room temperature for about 40 minutes.
- Take golf ball sized piece of the dough and roll into an oval shape.

- Repeat with the remaining dough. (Cover the oval pieces with the kitchen towel while preparing the remaining dough).
- Now, stretch the each oval into a tail shape, thinning and enlarging them.
- In a deep fryer, heat about 1/4-inchesof the oil to 385 degrees F and fry the dough pieces in batches tilll golden brown.
- Transfer the dough pieces onto paper towel lined plate to drain.
- In a large shallow dish, place the sugar and roll the dough pieces it it evenly.
- Serve with a topping of your favorite jam.

Amount per serving: 1

Timing Information:

| Preparation | 30 mins |
| Total Time | 2 hrs 30 mins |

Nutritional Information:

Calories	160.4
Fat	4.8g
Cholesterol	20.3mg
Sodium	188.7mg
Carbohydrates	24.6g
Protein	4.1g

* Percent Daily Values are based on a 2,000 calorie diet.

Summertime Beet Soup

Ingredients

- 1 (16 oz.) cans whole beets, undrained
- 1 (10 3/4 oz.) cans chicken broth, undiluted
- 1 (8 oz.) cartons sour cream
- 1/8 tsp white pepper
- 1 1/2 tsp lemon juice
- 2 tbsp chopped chives

Directions

- In a food processor, add broth and beets and pulse till smooth.
- In a large bowl, add the beet puree and the remaining ingredients except chives and stir to combine.
- Cover and refrigerate to chill before serving.
- Serve with a garnishing of the chives.

Amount per serving: 1

Timing Information:

| Preparation | 10 mins |
| Total Time | 10 mins |

Nutritional Information:

Calories	179.9
Fat	12.4g
Cholesterol	31.1mg
Sodium	386.7mg
Carbohydrates	13.6g
Protein	4.8g

* Percent Daily Values are based on a 2,000 calorie diet.

Old-Fashioned Dumplings

Ingredients

Dough

- 1 egg
- 4 C. flour
- 1/2 tsp salt
- 1 1/4 C. water
- 1/2 C. milk

Filling

- potato, peeled and cubed
- 1 (13 1/4 oz.) packages medium cheese, shredded
- 2 medium onions, chopped and cooked
- 1 tbsp butter
- 1 tsp white pepper
- salt

Directions

- For the dough in a large bowl, mix together the egg, milk and water.
- Slowly, add the flour and mix till well combined and a dough forms.
- Place the dough onto a floured surface and knead till an elastic dough forms.
- With a plastic wrap, cover the dough and keep in the warm place for about 1-2 hours.
- Place the dough onto a floured surface and roll like a pasta crust.
- For filling in a large pan of boiling water, cook the potatoes till tender enough.
- Drain well and transfer into a bowl.
- In a skillet melt the butter and sauté the onion till tender.

- Transfer the onion into the bowl with the potatoes.
- Add the cheese, salt and black pepper and with a potato masher, mash the mixture completely.
- Cut the crust in 2-inch circles and top with about 1 tsp of the filling.
- Fold the each crust in half and with your hands, pinch the edges
- In a pan of salted boiling water, cook the dumplings for about 4-5 minute.
- Through a colander, strain the dumplings and rinse under cold water.
- Drain completely.
- Serve hot with a topping of the sour cream.

Amount per serving: 8

Timing Information:

| Preparation | 2 hrs |
| Total Time | 2 hrs 45 mins |

Nutritional Information:

Calories	425.9
Fat	14.7g
Cholesterol	59.1mg
Sodium	630.5mg
Carbohydrates	55.1g
Protein	17.3g

* Percent Daily Values are based on a 2,000 calorie diet.

Wonderful Cabbage Casserole

Ingredients

- 1 1/2 C. long grain white rice, uncooked
- 1 C. chopped onion
- 1 (14 oz.) cans stewed tomatoes (with juice)
- 3 bacon, slices cooked crisp and crumbled
- 5 C. shredded cabbage
- 1 tsp sugar
- 1 tsp salt
- 1/2 tsp pepper
- 1 (19 oz.) cans tomato juice

Directions

- Set your oven to 350 degrees F before doing anything else and grease a large casserole dish.
- In a large bowl, add all the ingredients and mix till well combined.
- Cover and cook in the oven for about 45-60 minutes.
- Uncover the dish and cook in the oven for about 30 minutes, stirring once after 15 minutes.

Amount per serving: 8

Timing Information:

| Preparation | 15 mins |
| Total Time | 1 hr 45 mins |

Nutritional Information:

Calories	173.5
Fat	0.4g
Cholesterol	0.0mg
Sodium	605.3mg
Carbohydrates	39.0g
Protein	4.3g

* Percent Daily Values are based on a 2,000 calorie diet.

Quintessential Canadian Tarts

Ingredients

Shells

- 1 1/2 C. all-purpose flour
- 1/2 tsp sugar
- 1/4 tsp salt
- 4 1/2 tbsp cold butter, cut into bits
- 2 tbsp cold vegetable shortening

Filling

- 1 large egg, beaten lightly
- 1 tsp vanilla
- 1/4 C. butter, melted and cooled
- 1 C. firmly packed brown sugar
- 1 tbsp distilled white vinegar
- 1/4 C. raisins

Directions

- For shells in a food processor, add all the ingredients and pulse till a coarse meal forms.
- Place the mixture in a large bowl.
- Add enough chilled water and mix till a dough forms.
- Place the dough onto a floured surface and knead it briefly.
- With a plastic wrap, cover the dough and keep aside for about 1 hour.
- Place the dough onto the floured surface and roll to 3/8-inch thickness.
- Cut the rolled dough into 4 1/2-inch rounds and arrange into muffin cups.
- For the filling in a bowl, add the egg, butter and vanilla and beat till well combined.

- Add the vinegar, brown sugar and raisins and stir to combine.
- Place the filling into the pie shells and cook in the oven for about 15 minutes.
- Remove from the oven and keep aside on rack for about 5 minutes.
- Remove from the muffin cups and keep aside to cool completely.

Amount per serving: 1

Timing Information:

Preparation	20 mins
Total Time	35 mins

Nutritional Information:

Calories	224.9
Fat	10.8g
Cholesterol	39.2mg
Sodium	119.7mg
Carbohydrates	30.0g
Protein	2.2g

* Percent Daily Values are based on a 2,000 calorie diet.

Authentic Salmon Jerky

Ingredients

- 2 lbs salmon, cut into 1/4-inch thick strips
- 1/2 C. soy sauce
- 2 tbsp brown sugar
- 1/2 tsp fresh ginger
- 1/4 tsp pepper
- 1 tsp liquid smoke

Directions

- In a pan, mix together all the ingredients except salmon and bring to a boil.
- Remove from the heat and keep aside to cool.
- Add the salmon strips and marinate for about 15-60 minutes.
- Set your oven to 150 degrees F.
- Dry the salmon strips in the oven for about 5-6 hours.
- You can preserve these strips in airtight jars.

Amount per serving: 24

Timing Information:

Preparation	6 hrs
Total Time	6 hrs 10 mins

Nutritional Information:

Calories	56.0
Fat	1.6g
Cholesterol	17.3mg
Sodium	363.8mg
Carbohydrates	1.4g
Protein	8.3g

* Percent Daily Values are based on a 2,000 calorie diet.

Springtime Lemony Fiddleheads

Ingredients

- 2 C. fiddleheads (washed well and trimmed of brown spots)
- 1 C. water
- 1 tsp salt
- 1 tbsp olive oil
- 1 tbsp lemon juice
- 1/4 tsp black pepper
- salt

Directions

- In a pan, add the fiddleheads, water and bring to a boil.
- Reduce the heat and simmer for about 20 minutes.
- Drain the water and stir in the remaining ingredients.

Amount per serving: 4

Timing Information:

| Preparation | 5 mins |
| Total Time | 25 mins |

Nutritional Information:

Calories	31.1
Fat	3.3g
Cholesterol	0.0mg
Sodium	582.7mg
Carbohydrates	0.4g
Protein	0.0g

* Percent Daily Values are based on a 2,000 calorie diet.

Traditional Newfoundland Meal

- 2 hard bread cakes, split horizontally
- 1 pound salt cod steaks, skinned and cut into 1/2-inch strips
- 1 teaspoon salt
- 1/2 pound fatback, diced

Directions

- In a large bowl of cold water, soak the bread, covered for overnight.
- In a large pan of water, soak the cod, covered for overnight.
- Place the salt in the pan of bread and bring to a boil on medium-low heat.
- Simmer for about 2 minutes and drain well.
- Keep aside covered to keep it warm.
- Now, change the water of the cod and bring to a boil.
- Simmer for about 20 minutes and drain well.
- Remove the bones from the fish and add in the pan with the warm bread.
- In a frying pan, cook the fatback for about 10 minutes on medium heat.
- Transfer the fatback and pan dripping in the pan with the bread and cod.
- Gently, stir to combine and serve immediately.

Amount per serving: 4

Timing Information:

Preparation	15 m
Total Time	35 m

Nutritional Information:

Calories	930
Fat	53.2g
Cholesterol	30.5g
Sodium	205mg
Carbohydrates	8763mg
Protein	76.5g

* Percent Daily Values are based on a 2,000 calorie diet.

Family Feast Apple Crisp

Ingredients

- 6 C. sliced peeled apples
- 1/4 C. sugar
- 2 tbsp lemon juice
- 3/4 C. rolled oats
- 1/2 C. brown sugar
- 1/2 C. flour
- 1 tsp ground cinnamon
- 1/3 C. butter

Directions

- Set your oven to 350 degrees F before doing anything and lightly, grease a casserole dish.
- In the prepared casserole dish, arrange the apple slices and sprinkle with the sugar.
- Drizzle with the lemon juice evenly.
- In a bowl, mix together the oats, flour, brown sugar and cinnamon.
- With a pastry cutter, cut the butter and mix till a crumbly mixture forms.
- Place the crumb mixture over apple slices and cook in the oven for about 40 minutes.
- Serve warm.

Amount per serving: 6

Timing Information:

Preparation	15 mins
Total Time	55 mins

Nutritional Information:

Calories	335.7
Fat	11.2g
Cholesterol	27.0mg
Sodium	97.3mg
Carbohydrates	59.0g
Protein	2.9g

* Percent Daily Values are based on a 2,000 calorie diet.

Thanks for Reading! Now Let's Try some Sushi and Dump Dinners....

http://bit.ly/2443TFg

To grab this **box set** simply follow the link mentioned above, or tap the book cover.

This will take you to a page where you can simply enter your email address and a PDF version of the **box set** will be emailed to you.

I hope you are ready for some serious cooking!

http://bit.ly/2443TFg

You will also receive updates about all my new books when they are free.

Also don't forget to like and subscribe on the social networks. I love meeting my readers. Links to all my profiles are below so please click and connect :)

Facebook

Twitter

Come On...
Let's Be Friends :)

I adore my readers and love connecting with them socially. Please follow the links below so we can connect on Facebook, Twitter, and Google+.

Facebook

Twitter

I also have a blog that I regularly update for my readers so check it out below.

My Blog

Can I Ask A Favour?

If you found this book interesting, or have otherwise found any benefit in it. Then may I ask that you post a review of it on Amazon? Nothing excites me more than new reviews, especially reviews which suggest new topics for writing. I do read all reviews and I always factor feedback into my newer works.

So if you are willing to take ten minutes to write what you sincerely thought about this book then please visit our Amazon page and post your opinions.

Again thank you!

INTERESTED IN OTHER EASY COOKBOOKS?

Everything is easy! Check out my Amazon Author page for more great cookbooks:

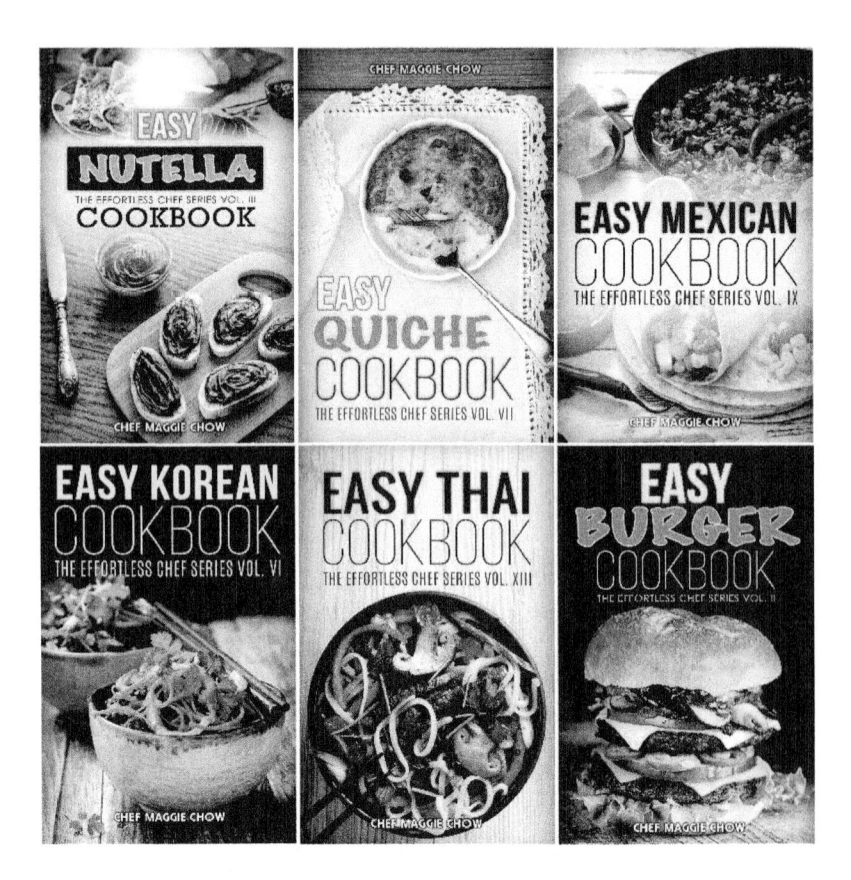

For a complete listing of all my books please see my author page at:

http://amazon.com/author/maggiechow

Printed in Great Britain
by Amazon